Raving at the Big Bad

Lucas Modzelewski

BookLeaf Publishing
India | USA | UK

Presentation by *BookLeaf Publishing*

Web: www.bookleafpub.com

E-mail: info@bookleafpub.com

ISBN: 9789357448710

First edition 2022

ACKNOWLEDGEMENT

Thanks to: my parents, brothers, Kim and Lennon.

for Kim

so you know

I'm still trying

sunscreen

When I think about all the things
that I can do
to save the world
I like to think outside of the coffin
and wear sunscreen
so that
others don't get burned
by the sun.

And I do this as a reminder
that I do my part
to bravely face the sun
and to save the world
from ultraviolet death
even though we can't see ultraviolet
and the word itself has an alluring beauty
that probably nobody else sees but me
since I understand everything
about ultraviolet
and feel no guilt for guilting those
who don't wear white cream
to protect me
from the burns of the sun.

What nobler thing is there

than to defeat death
for your fellow civilians
by rubbing it in their face
and all over their skin.

Some people get burned
some don't
some might
some want to be
some get burned by things other than the sun
although the sun is blamed
and some don't get burned at all but display
the symptoms of being burned
and keep people in fear
of daylight.

But it's all the same
selfish people are going to burn
but burn differently to those who burn in the
shade
and so, when I think about what I can do
all I know is that to help myself
is to help others
because we're all in this together
because there's nothing safe under the sun.

I see an orange skank
all tanned
all made-up

platinum hair
big lips for the kissing
huge fake tits
and an ugly, little dog
of the Chihuahua or Pomeranian breed
and I think, "how dare you"
and I think, "how insensitive"
and I think, "the sun is killing everyone"
and I think,
"the sun is killing you, I better slap some more
on
myself
for both of our protection"
and I think, "screw you.
This wouldn't have happened if you
stayed the fuck at home!"

death

It's a cruel truth that life
is so out of sync with death
in that death forgives you
and life doesn't.

Death makes those
who were inconvenienced by your life
want you back alive
and life just says,
"fuck you, you're alive, be alive or dead
I don't care!"

Death perhaps gives you
spectacularly
what you wanted
and that is for pretty ladies
or handsome men
to think about you
and for people to stop
hang out for a bit
and whisper nice things to you.

But you can't enjoy it.

And what's worse

you can't flirt
with that attractive person
looking at
your corpse
and life just stands there laughing,
"haha, you will never fuck this person
you will never fuck anything again
you are dead!"

Provided you weren't
a real piece of shit
death does you some favours:
you can lay around and do nothing all day
and after awhile
you go from great
to legendary
to genius
and in a few generations more:
genius
to
prophet.

However
if you were
a real piece of shit
then I suppose
death does you no favours
and I guess
death is as mean as life.

dancing in an op shop

Thursday, 7 November 2013
I was at the Brotherhood of St. Lawrence
in Melbourne CBD
flipping through second-hand clothing
when this dark guy
and his curly-haired friend
Tara
stood really close to me.

Tara started dancing
to a song on the radio
uncomfortably in my space.
To diffuse the awkwardness
I started dancing with her
to which she turned around
and laughed
and the guy laughed,
"stop flirting Tara!"
and then she said to me,
"that's okay, you're gorgeous!"
and I laughed it off
and threw a few more dance moves

at her:
here's the pepper mill: crack-crack-crack,
here's the butcher: slice-slice-slice,
and Tara joined in
but really engaged those hip-thrusting motions
in a fervent
but non-sexual way.
I smiled and went home happy.

And I remember that memory
very well
because every now and then
in an argument with Kim
she would take that innocent memory
and say
"oh, you want the house clean?!"
"oh, you want the dishes done?!"
"oh, you want attention?!"
"oh, you feel neglected?!"
"oh, you're burned out?!"
"oh, you're hungry?!"
"oh, you're bored?!"
"oh, you're hungover?!"
"oh, you're depressed?!"
"oh, you want to kill yourself?!"
"oh, you're hallucinating because of alcohol withdrawals?!"
"oh, you just had your appendix removed?!"
"oh, your grandmother just died?!"

"oh, you want to hold my hand?!"

"…well, why don't you just go DANCE
with some BITCH
at an op shop
INSTEAD?!"

asbestos

You've got asbestos in the heart
for enclosing it
in a drywall
so that nobody
gets to it.

Every time
I yell into the plaster
to get you to listen
you mock me
and bate me to get to it
by smashing my way through.

But I can't do that
because I just couldn't
hence
you win
because I'm screaming at a wall
that I will never break
that I'm not strong enough to rupture
and that I wouldn't even put
posters of naked ladies
calendars
mindfulness tips
or eviction notices
on.

legacy

What good is it
to be a bastard in life
and to suffer for the redemption
of a legacy
that is to speak on your behalf
all the reasons why you couldn't be happy
or pleasant
or patient
or decent
in the company of those that loved you
whilst in the world of the living.

For if you couldn't
build that legacy
to apologise to those you hurt
the legacy itself
is your cruelty
and anything good:
a confusing anomaly.

nasty neighbour

I remember when I was a kid
my mother got into a feud
with the woman next door
for stalking my brother
home
after school
which ignited
the apocalypse.

And therefore
by loyalty
my side was decided for life.

I must say
that neighbour
was a cunt
and that I was on the right side
because that ginger-haired
flabby
ho
had a reputation
amongst her own ashamed family
to fuck with people
and admitted
that she wanted

to murder
mum.
According to her family's words
she wanted someone to
"do her in".

I had a friend named Joseph
who was my age
10 or something
who said
"if she does anything
I will help you."
Now that's a good friend.
I wonder if I kept being his friend
even when he was
uncomfortably
spanking my ass
in a gay way
that he would stop doing
gay things
that made me uncomfortable
and grow out of
sexually
harassing
other boys.

The ho's son
was a beady-eyed fuck
and my brother and I

gave him shit
for never being able
to blink
because it was the least we could do.

And it pissed me off
that when I was about 14
he somehow bought
porn magazines
and yet I didn't have
connections
to buy my own
porn magazines
which was perhaps my first brush with
failure.

It gives me no satisfaction
that once
when my mother was attending
a doctor's appointment
she witnessed some retard crying,
"oh no, I dropped my baby!
I dropped my baby!"
before realising
it was
our favourite
murderous
next-door neighbour.

It gives us no satisfaction
that after all grief
this woman drops
this new kid
that came out of her.
But it gives me satisfaction
that my dog Milo
barked
and scared her fat, hairy boyfriend
off his motorcycle
and noone cares that dad had to pay
for damages
because it was
really
satisfying
which I think we all
agreed.

creation's secret

I'd say it's impolite
if you spill your blood
or the blood of others
and not think of those genetic
hand-written notes of God
contained within the smears
clots
and stains
of our DNA
saying, "Hello, my children.
This is YHWH,
the one true Lord.
You have found Creation's secret.
Now share it peacefully with the world,"
as it turns brown on a tissue
or gets washed off some cop's nightstick
or vomited up from a stomach ulcer
or in Stalin's brain when he had a stroke
or patted dry when squeezing a pimple too hard
or when murdering someone
or being in a car accident
or when pricking your finger to monitor
gestational diabetes
or cutting words or phrases or names or symbols
into your flesh

with sharp objects
or when wiping your ass too hard with rough toilet paper
or cleaning and dressing a kid's knee after falling over.

You oughta remember
that in your blood
is the alphabet of existence
the language of Creation
the manuscript of God
where
the good Lord
says
hello.

opinions

I wish I had a selective sense of smell
because your opinions
are like farts
whose impact is supposed to be finite
yet it lingers around and gets on my skin
on my clothes
and in my moustache hair.

It gets stuck on me
I take it around
I can't bear it
eyes water
I try to breathe out of my mouth
but my mouth is too close
to my moustache hair
and so, instead, I taste it.
And what's that grumbling sound I hear?
You're whipping up some more.

road of perdition

We'll call him Roger
and he ran
the Basin Music Festival Youth Stage.

It was my first gig
mum and dad watching
recording
with a video camera
that required
tapes.

We plodded on stage
didn't know what to do
and got set-up quicker than anyone
expected.

We launched into our first song
which was once called
"Who You Are"
and then later
"Road of Perdition"
because to a 14-year-old
that sounded cooler.

There we were playing
“Road of Perdition”
and apparently, we’d started before
they were ready for us
and I could see
this Roger guy
shaking his head
and doing that cut-throat motion
as in “nope
stop
cut it out”
but fuck you, Roger
we kept playing
“Road of Perdition”
to the very end.

My parents clapped for me
before they were divorced.
They would always support
my music, they said
all the way until
the car ride home.

I still recall
when you did that
cut-throat motion
how your natural chin
would squish against
a fatty reserve

of neck-flap
that one might say
was an additional chin
but all I can say
is that I remember
all those supposed chins
squished up against one another
shaming me
for playing music like “Road of Perdition”
too early.

noise complaints

Michaela likes
to ruin our lives
by calling the cops
when we think
too loud.

We know it's you
because when Kim and I
are in the kitchen
whispering above a certain level
your window opens
curtains ruffle
and then cops show up
wanting my details
Kim's details
Lennon's details
all because this woman's husband
left because he didn't wanna
fuck her
and now she's fuckless
and upset.

I explain how someone screamed
on our TV.

I explain how I sneezed because
of shaking white pepper
on a hard-boiled egg.

I explain it wasn't even
human voices
but the sound
of Tibetan singing bowls.

I explain that my smoke alarm
was alerting me
to change its battery.

I explain that it is Easter
and I was leading
the family prayer.

I explain that it was actually
a cloud of bats
screeching over my house
mid-flight.

Then
I look at those cops in their facemasks
thinking,
"you're fucking retards"
"I can take you"
"sex is supposed to be loud"
but instead say,

“we’re okay, thanks”
“have a nice day”
and then wind down my window,
“fuck you, nosy neighbour!”
and Kim,
“fuck you, nosy neighbour!”

I’m certain
I cannot rely on such a person
to raise the alarm
when I’m dying of a heart attack
if I do not first make
offensive noise
when dying.

white chocolate frogs

Harry was
a good friend to have
because his mum was French
and said his dad died
in a car crash
so, she bought Harry a lot of stuff
and being his best friend for
those couple of years
I got some stuff as well
like white chocolate frogs
from the canteen
at school.
Mrs Ferguson said
“are you buying friends, Harry?”
he said “no”
but he certainly was
and for that day
bought me.

He was pretty good
at making up games
said people like Lathan Van Trout

who called it a gift
"he has a gift"
which offended me
because I wanted a gift too
and if anything
the gift
was in Lathan Van Trout's hands
in the form
of white chocolate frogs.

In my adulthood
I'm starting to think
that his
dad
dying
in a car crash
was bullshit.

before you go into the drink

I have strong beliefs
that are important to me.

I know
sharing it
doesn't make a difference
and it'll never
change the world.

But some things I just don't take lightly
and I try to live
for freedom
and suffer
to know uncomfortable truths.

It's my solace to know
that even if knowledge can't save anything
you can go down
tearing wool from your eyes
knowing a killer didn't fool you
that you saw everything
and that they don't own

the thoughts
and perception
you have
of them.

It's the ultimate
self-love
to say to yourself
when crushed into shit,
"I still know".

It's just sad
standing on the Titanic
iceberg ahead
screaming
pointing
raving at the big bad
(knowing you can't scream the ship around
or the iceberg into the deep)
that you just want your friends and family
to know
and share those moments with them
before you go into the drink.

It's perhaps
more crushing than the tyrant
that those loved ones won't
join you
until you're all indiscriminate

floating bodies
in the frozen water.

The dead body is buoyant
but it’s that
which makes you sink.

withdrawals

"I don't want a gravestone with a picture
…not of my smiling face."

I think this as electricity jolts through my brain
and very little space in my skull
to contain it.

You get up
and feel as if the earth is tilted on a different axis
pulling your drunken ass sooner to the grave
to get your death over with.

The first day is fine, you drink all night.
What you shouldn't do
is wake up early in the morning
to finish the bottle.
That's the big mistake.
Because by the time you finish the bottle
it's 7am
people are waking up
and now you find your sober-clock
has reset once more
and you will deteriorate
back into a hangover
while conscious

sometime during the hellish day.

Although you don't feel
as shit as you did
when puking at 3am
you know that you'll have to wait
to 10am
for the bottle shop to open.

Yes, you've already decided
you'll break your promise to your wife
to not continue the day after
although
you already broke the first promise
by relapsing.

"She'll forgive you again"
you think.

You're drunk but playful
buttering her up to soften the blow
when you order more.
You make excuses to yourself
to follow through:
"it's just to chase the hangover"
"you're in control"
"you'll nurse it"
"you'll pace yourself".

This is the second day.
Now, you're good as long as you don't
carry over to a third day.
You'll just have a hangover
tomorrow
and that'll be it.
You won't withdraw.
You reassure yourself you'll stop today
"as long as there isn't more to drink
if you wake up sick and fucked at 3am"
so, you resolve to drink everything before late
evening
knowing the hangover
could do its thing
while you sleep
a normal night's duration.

But you pass out
before you finish it all
and wake at 3am to heave your wretched guts.
Your balls ache
your asshole hurts from involuntary clenching.
You spend the next few hours sipping
your remaining vodka
running to the toilet to vomit through your nose
shaking
throat shredded up
and your entire torso crippled from constriction.
You lay back down

unsure if you're sleeping or half-awake.
Your wife has already spent the night on the couch
and there's no way
you're getting hangover sex.
For some reason
you still think she's approachable for sex
at 4am
and wonder whether or not
if you'd just go into the room, you'd start fucking.
You don't bother.
But you're alone so you can be shameless
you don't bother to wipe all the puke
out of your moustache
you leave your tears on the floor.
You sadly sip water out of your hands at the tap
avoiding your reflection in the mirror
because you know you're so fucked;
blood shot
dizzy
kooky eyes
trying to look back at you.

You've lost your shame
and dignity
knowing with terror
and anxiety
that day three looms.

You keep sipping your drink
but you're just not getting drunker.
Then, with the last sip
you feel warm inside again
and wanna stay that way.

Time has made no sense all night;
it's 3am
and you spend what feels like hours of suffering
although when you check the time next
it's only 3:13.

And then you twist
and shake
and kick
and it's 4:37.

And finally
all hope in regeneration through sleep
is lost when dawn breaks.
The bottle is empty.
You swear you're done but the will is weak
when you suffer for the next three hours
until bottle shops open again.
You don't plan to butter up the wife this time
you order in secret and creep out the front door
or you just grumble
and do it
even though it upsets her.

You still hope for sex.

Day three is sometimes
the easiest to be drunk on.
It's also the day you least remember.
You drink quicker and harder
and feel warm and sound
the shakes are gone
you manage to eat
but you sense
you've defeated yourself.

Hours later
you're cross-eyed
your teeth are covered in putrid foam
your lips are cracked and scabbed
your red face a caked, oily, blotchy, puffy failure
of innocence
you're covered in bruises
you've chipped a toenail somehow
and artificially, you're happy about it.
You spend the day in bed
listening to music
watching YouTube
and jerking off.

You're in a temporary
artificially-distilled

happy place.
Nostalgia about what you were
what you wanted
what you loved about yourself
ferment warmly and intensely
in your toxic, tinny blood.
In your most disrespectable state
you briefly – somehow – find a self-respect
that eludes you
that evaporates
in sobriety.

You're nearing the end of your capacity.
The body writhes to purge itself by early day
four.
You are unquenchably thirsty
you stomach no food, food is an abomination
you know you're dehydrated
and hungry
and try to fill your stomach
with the neutrality of water
hoping that'll keep away
the evil hunger for food
the body knows it can't hold.
But your hunger isn't abated by the water
acid reflux gurgles up your injured throat
and singes the raw oesophageal tissues.
Your Adam's apple dislocates from retching.
Your body's a floppy, useless mess

you can't lift or carry anything
not even a cup.
Your jaw doesn't work, it won't chew food
the mouth doesn't want to move
your lips tremble unnaturally
no muscles in your body have done anything for days.

You have a choice to make…
to stop now
or push through with just one more
…one more day of drinking.

You know your reality;
you're not sleeping, not meaningfully
you've peaked in drunkenness
and can no longer physically get
any drunker
without dying
and it's with the gnashing of teeth
and remorse
that you know
you're now chemically hooked.
You're drinking purely to not die
to just bring your brain up
and satiate it
lest you withdraw the moment it calls for a fix.

You bastard.

You know all this.

And by early day five
1:30 in the morning
you're overwhelmed by palpitations
your breathing's shallow
you hear things that aren't there.
You are a crippled sack of weak shit.
Uselessly alive.
If someone broke into your house
they could throw a paper plane at you
and you will die
from discombobulation alone.

For the next 8 days you will suffer.
You'll get better on day two
and curiously get worse on day three or four
with the most demented withdrawals
imaginable.
You're painfully bloated and it's laborious to
urinate.
Your body is too thirsty for its swollen capacity
its ability to process the water
and fluids you drink
has greatly decelerated.
You desperately want to piss
so you can drink more fluids
although your urine stream is brown

hot
stinging
and your penis
has all but retracted into your body
your foreskin hanging half-empty.
If you've happened
to retain any food to even digest
your shit smells like pure nail polish remover.
You're a confused blend of hot and cold
and you're punished
and tortured
by the tireless absence of rest.

Again, time is disorderly;
it's slow and fast
and you're only half-asleep the majority of the night.
You feel your body drift
into a desperately desired beginning of a sleep cycle
and being consciously aware of that
you're roused back to consciousness
and have to start over.
When you do get moments of sleep
you suffer from
dreadful
demonic
grotesque dreams;
interdimensional beings chasing you

through geometrical shapes
in incomprehensible, bottomless realms
or the universe collapsing in on itself
in a never-ending
impenetrable
vacuous darkness
or spiders and crab-like bugs crawling on your
skin
or murderous maniacs
thrusting chainsaws through your spine
and carving box cutters
across your forehead.

You wake up with night sweats
having to change your pajamas multiple times.
Wet but shivering from the cold
as if someone doused you with water
your only blanket is drenched
and you must stand there shivering
waiting for your sweaty blanket to dry
in real time.
You need to find a way to stay warm
and dry
but also cool because your face flushes hot.

The insides of your ears are a gloopy mess.
And when you finally decide to brush your teeth
for the first time in 5 or 6 or 7 days
it's of little use.

Your breath will stink for today
the next day
and the next
it literally smells worse than your ass.
Your gums bleed at the smallest touch.
Your skin is covered in a film of grease
but your body is still too weak
and sensitive
to the bear the water
of a shower.

When, at last, you wash
you burn and shake
because your temperature fluctuates.
Regardless how much you wash your crotch
it won't suffice
after being bedridden in a drunken stupor
the better part of a week.
You wipe your face with the part of the towel
that was just between your cheeks
and get hit by the funky waft
of a stubborn stench
refusing to budge from thorough swipes
of the soap bar through your ass
and from body wash as well.

Again
sleep will flee from you.
Again

sweat will drown you.
Your appetite will come back with a vengeance
you'll crave random things
like canned tomatoes
microwaved potatoes
uncooked bread dough
raw fish
grapes
things with cheese
Plain noodles
uncooked eggs
avocados
and eventually
raw vegetables.

You realise
when you do this time and time again
that's 5 days of drinking
plus 8 days of recovering
and 2-3
(though occasionally 6 weeks)
of "getting on top of things" once more.

Half a month is spent
on the piss and recovery
the other part is trying to have a normal life
of responsibility and productivity.
Then you go into the next month
a grumpy bastard

until you do it
again.

There're really not enough
months in a year
or years in a lifetime
to not become
a ruined avatar
of a thing
that used to laugh
smile
love
dream
and
try.

artist

Ultimately
it was a nice lesson
to have to throw away
my drawings
and paintings
from school
because they were “mess”
so as an adult
I would not get
attached to a piece
but instead leave it behind
as soon as I made it
not ever knowing
if
it
had
some
value
because I was
far gone
doing the next thing
and the next
and the next
lest I get caught
by

desperation
to want to keep it.

It is how I became an artist
and
also
impoverished.

toys

As a young boy
I wasn't allowed
to leave the house
because
everyone
were rapists
and wanted
my ass
said mum.

The world was denied
my discovery
but I was amused
by an ensemble
of great toys
to which was my consolation
and friends
who absorbed
my tears
and snot
into their fabric epidermises
and polyester guts
to hush my fears
from the fighting
outside my door.

Getting older
I couldn't quite will
the personhood into my toys
like once before
but the rapists were still in the world
and I had to withdraw
my complaints
of isolation
and curiosity
and say
"thank you for
my brand-new school books
I take it all back"
so I can better neglect
Indonesian classes
more than those less fortunate
than me.

Those toys would smile knowing
when 18 or 19
I used the stove
for the first time
to make bacon
or something
and have been dodging rapists
ever since.

what a great person

For a drunk
the easiest way in the world
to feel better than everybody else
besides getting drunk
is to allocate one day a year
to audacious sobriety.

Yes.

New Year's Eve.

Because while people are
getting drunk
you're just there
being good
being strangely temperate
being sensible and innocent
being sound of mind
being able to make reasonable choices
being a designated driver
being some loser's therapist
being the person that gives some skank
water instead of yuck dick
being able to pick up your trash

and your party popper streamers
being able to restrain yourself
from shouting “woo!”
and “fuck yeah!”
like an asshole
being able to walk
being able to eat breakfast
and go for a jog the morning after
being able to justify feeling better
than that fist-pumping bastard
who is big
and who has shaved sides of their head
and who has weird sunglasses
and who has an abnormally high voice
from steroid use
and people look at you
in all your unusual and glorious sobriety
and think,
“wow. what a great person.”

But then of course
go back to normal.

Not the next day but
Jan 2nd or 3rd.

That’s a respectable New Year’s gap
for getting pissed
as always.

peace

Peace is having respect for happiness
and remembrance of joy
even when
it's died.

It is to possess sad things
but not give up
and not curse things
and not kill one's self.

For example
when Kim was pregnant
with the twins
I was happy.

And telling my mother
and seeing her happy
made me happy.

And getting brochures
at the doctor's office
made me happy.

And buying
'baby on board' signs

made me happy.

But to not hear their heartbeats
made me nervous.

To see they weren't growing
made me question.

And to watch Kim
standing in line
at the emergency department
clutching her stomach
but sensibly waiting
like she was buying
an almond milk chai latte
made me retch.

Then to bring her home
and watch her flush
our babies
in a pool of blood
and gunk
down the toilet
broke my heart.

Yet I don't disqualify
said happiness
though it was captured
by the blues.

It still makes me happy
that that made me happy
and it never occurred to me
(or if it did, I've forgotten)
to give up.

What a marvellous feeling
it is
when you
forget to give up.

You'll sometimes find
when walking through
your dark, swampy psyche
expecting to wallow
to dwell
that peace has let itself in
is lounging freely on your sofa
with its feet on your coffee table
and its shoes all over
your nice table cloths
saying,
"nice place you've got here!"

And you wonder how
or when
it got in.

i believe you

There's no global catastrophe;
not pandemic
nor natural disaster
economic collapse
or government takeover
that takes priority
over holding you
in my arms
when you smile
and ask for peanut butter
and rub noses
and do funny faces
that must be reciprocated
before we do something else.

When I say,
"I love you, Lennon"
and you say,
"lahlee, daddy"
I know I've achieved
my life's destiny
to be content
happy
and okay
because

I believe you.

From the sound of your heart
drumming at 170 beats per minute
at 8 weeks old
racing to birth
to meet us

or when you stopped crying
opened your eyes
and looked at me
when I said,
"hello, my little boy!"
as soon as you
were born

or the first thing
to make you smile on command
was to be told,
"I love you"
and me knowing
you believe me

or when you'd need me
to tuck you in
one blanket at a time:
"do you want your first blanket?"
"gah" (yes)
"do you want your second blanket?"

"gah"
"do you want your…third blanket?"
"gah"
"do you want your…last blanket?"
"gah!"

It's things like this
that make me believe you
when you say
"lahlee".

And it's because of these reasons
I hold you forever
though the world may be obliterated
or worse
your pants keep releasing
wafts of shit
that smell of pure garbage
or like the alleyway dumpster
of a Chinese restaurant
right in my face.

boss

Shitin called me
when I was on
a homemade life-support rig
recovering from work
wondering why
I turned down work the next day
as a casual employee.

“NO”
“do it yourself”
“I work my ass off for you”
“I’ll come to work
when my fucking
toe nails
and fingernails
grow back”.

When you work 8 days in a row
for Shitin
though company policy limits it to 5
for safety reasons
and when you push trolleys
for 10 hours
without a break
for Shitin

though you're entitled
to an hour and a half
and when Shitin tells you
you will get your own store
a full-time contract
with annual leave
sick leave
and even paternity leave
then gives it
to one of his Indian friends
when your wife is heavily pregnant
I think it's fair to say
I don't owe you
Shitin.

Taking my wife
to her ultrasound in the morning
when my son is in breech
with umbilical cord around his neck
is good enough reason
to yell at you on the phone
on the street.

"I've covered your ass"
"I've done the shit hours"
"the shit jobs"
"you gave my store away!"
"YOU GAVE MY STORE AWAY!"

"I don't owe you
Shitin!"

"I DON'T OWE YOU
SHITIN."

embarrassment

People ought to be as persistent
as embarrassment
if they're driven to succeed
because some embarrassing things
never surrender
and replay in your head
the course of your natural life.

Like the time I was trying to form
an acoustic duo
in 2013
and met someone
who agreed to jam
without a setlist.

But when it happened
it went nowhere
and was awkward as fuck.

There I was
scrolling on Ultimate Guitar
trying to find chords for "God Only Knows".
I fumbled my way through it.
Who fucking chooses a Beach Boy's song
as the first song

to noodle through
when there's…what?
114 different chords
of add9 sus2 dim whatever# minor sus4 varieties
in an intro.

“what shall we play next?”

“gee I dunno
how about
Flight of the Bumblebee?”

“wow
let me just throw
this guitar
outta the window instead
and maybe it’ll smash
in the key of A minor
as Nikolai Rimsky-Korsakov
had intended”.

I felt like a chump behind an instrument
I prided myself
(at least back then)
at being good at.

"Fucking Beach Fucking Boys"
I thought

"I swear I can fucking play the fucking mother
fucking guitar"
I silently lamented
as I farted my way through
the Assholian scale.

I never saw her again
and although it was solely for music
I was offended
that she ghosted me.

I later realised
she ghosted me
because she thought
I was trying to fuck her.

That, I would never do.
(Kim: Why don't you just
DANCE with some BITCH
and play BEACH BOYS
with some OTHER BITCH
and FUCK EVERY ONE)

Right before she left
I asked, "you wanna drink?"
not thinking of anything of it.
She abruptly said, "oh no, I gotta go!"
pointing at the door.
"okay"

It dawned on me
that she thought I meant alcohol
as in,
"now we've got that music shit out the way
how about you and I get intoxicated
and fucking fuck
and just see what happens
when we fuck
of course".

It is the fictional scene
where I explain myself
that I obsess over the most
because I wasn't quick enough
to assert that I'm not
a creep:

"oh, not, like, alcohol or anything!
I'm sorry, man
it's just I realise I hadn't offered you anything
to eat or drink
the entire time"

I go on,
"I meant cordial
or milk
or Metamucil
or a Ribena rip-off
or WATER"

to which she would laugh
and assure me she knew what I meant
although really
deep down inside
totally thought
I wanted her.

Annie
if you're out there
I fucking meant
water.

ice cream

I've done worse things
but for some reason
when I think about one event
that I would change
I always come
to the same answer.

I was 12 years old
standing in line at a food court
with mum
waiting to buy
ice cream.

A woman with her baby
in a pram
was ahead of us
ready to go.

As she turned the pram around
her baby started crying
which the woman ignored
but I had seen
the baby's
toy rabbit
fall on the floor.

The child was distraught
helpless
reaching out
but the mother didn't see
so they went away.

I froze
like ice cream
"please somebody have seen that"
"please lady, turn around"
"it can't just be me"
but when I looked around
everybody was hypnotised
by the glowing
pink menu
above their heads.

It was just me.

Sometimes it'll be just you.

I swallowed my spit
sweated
grey rabbit on the ground
the lady and pram soon outta sight
and then nothing.

"here you go, love

here's your ice cream".

Wished I had a voice
wished I could move
wished I left the safety
of my mother's side
to help someone.

That could explain why
I live my life
to stand out of line
and make a scene
and look like an idiot
in the event that somebody needs me
to be brave enough
to turn my back on ice cream
and care.

www.ingramcontent.com/pod-product-compliance
Lightning Source LLC
Chambersburg PA
CBHW051735130826
49812CB00033B/868
* 9 7 8 9 3 5 7 4 4 8 7 1 0 *